HAL•LEONARD
INSTRUMENTAL PLAY-ALONG

ALTO SAX

Christmas SONGS

T0081625

CONTENTS

To access audio visit:
www.halleonard.com/mylibrary

Enter Code
6098-7416-0421-6558

Audio Arrangements by Peter Deneff

ISBN 978-1-4950-2554-9

HAL•LEONARD®
CORPORATION

7777 W. BLUEMOUND RD. P.O. BOX 13819 MILWAUKEE, WI 53213

Visit Hal Leonard Online at
www.halleonard.com

ALL I WANT FOR CHRISTMAS IS YOU

ALTO SAX

Words and Music by MARIAH CAREY
and WALTER AFANASIEFF

To Coda ✛

D.S. al Coda

CODA ✛

THE CHRISTMAS WALTZ

ALTO SAX

Words by SAMMY CAHN
Music by JULE STYNE

HAPPY HOLIDAY

from the Motion Picture Irving Berlin's HOLIDAY INN

ALTO SAX

Words and Music by
IRVING BERLIN

I WONDER AS I WANDER

ALTO SAX

By JOHN JACOB NILES

I'LL BE HOME FOR CHRISTMAS

ALTO SAX

Words and Music by KIM GANNON
and WALTER KENT

LET IT SNOW! LET IT SNOW! LET IT SNOW!

ALTO SAX

Words by SAMMY CAHN
Music by JULE STYNE

MARY, DID YOU KNOW?

ALTO SAX

Words and Music by MARK LOWRY
and BUDDY GREENE

THE MOST WONDERFUL TIME OF THE YEAR

ALTO SAX

Words and Music by EDDIE POLA
and GEORGE WYLE

MY FAVORITE THINGS

from THE SOUND OF MUSIC

ALTO SAX

Lyrics by OSCAR HAMMERSTEIN II
Music by RICHARD RODGERS

SILVER BELLS
from the Paramount Picture THE LEMON DROP KID

ALTO SAX

Words and Music by JAY LIVINGSTON
and RAY EVANS

THIS CHRISTMAS

ALTO SAX

Words and Music by DONNY HATHAWAY
and NADINE McKINNOR

WHITE CHRISTMAS
from the Motion Picture Irving Berlin's HOLIDAY INN

ALTO SAX

Words and Music by
IRVING BERLIN